THE CONDUCTOR

THE CONDUCTOR

THE THEORY OF HIS ART

EXTRAIT DU GRAND D'INSTRUMENTATION
ET D'ORCHESTRATION MODERNES

BY

HECTOR BERLIOZ

Translated by JOHN BROADHOUSE

WITH 41 DIAGRAMS AND EXAMPLES

WILLIAM REEVES   83 CHARING CROSS ROAD,
BOOKSELLER LIMITED   —— LONDON, W.C.2 ——

Republished 1976
Scholarly Press, Inc., 22929 Industrial Drive East
St. Clair Shores, Michigan 48080

Standard Book Number 403-00247-8
Library of Congress Catalog Card Number; 71-107160

This edition is printed on a high-quality,
acid-free paper that meets specification
requirements for fine book paper referred
to as "300-year" paper

THE CONDUCTOR:
THE THEORY OF HIS ART.
(LE CHEF D'ORCHESTRE, THEORIE DE SON ART.)

MUSIC seems to be the hardest to satisfy of all the arts, the most difficult to cultivate, and that of which the productions are the most rarely presented under conditions which permit of their real value being appreciated, of their nature being seen, and of an intimate idea of their true character being realised.

Of all productive artists, the composer is, as a matter of fact, almost the only one who depends on a crowd of intermediaries to bring his work before the public—intermediaries who may be intelligent or stupid, devoted or hostile, active or inert, and who yet have it in their power, from the first moment to the last, to contribute to illuminate it on the one hand, or, on the other, to disfigure, calumniate, or even destroy it altogether.

Singers are often accused of being the most dangerous of these intermediaries; but I believe the accusation is wrong. The most formidable of them

all, in my opinion, is the conductor. A bad singer
only damages his own part; the incapable or malevolent conductor ruins everything. Happy to some
extent is the composer when the conductor into
whose hands he falls is not, at the same time, both
incapable and malevolent; for nothing can resist an
influence so pernicious. Under such circumstances
the most wonderful orchestra is paralysed; the
finest singers are annoyed and benumbed; there is
neither spirit nor unity. Under such direction the
noblest flights of the author seem but folly, enthu-
siasm has all the heart knocked out of it, inspiration
is thrown violently to the ground, the angel no
longer has wings, the man of genius becomes a
madman or a fool, the divine statue is hurled from
its pedestal and dragged in the mud; and, worse
than all, the public, and the most highly cultivated
musical audience, find it impossible, in the case of a
new work heard for the first time, to recognise the
ravages committed by the conductor, or to discover
the follies, the faults, and the crimes of which he
is guilty.*

* Weingartner, in his brochure, "On Conducting,"
quotes this entire paragraph from Berlioz, and adds this
significant comment: "What experiences Berlioz must
have had for this wild cry to be drawn from him can be
estimated from the single fact that a conductor who in the
first half of the nineteenth century occupied a really fore-

If certain faults of execution are noted, it is not upon him, but upon his victims, that the responsibility is cast. If he causes a wrong entry of the chorus in a finale, if he sets up a discordant balance between chorus and orchestra, or between the two extreme sides of the instrumental group, if he has foolishly precipitated or delayed a movement, if he has interrupted a singer before the end of a phrase, the verdict is—the singers are detestable, the orchestra did not hold together, the violins spoilt the principal passage, there was no " go " in anything, the tenor failed and did not know his part, the harmony was confused, the author did not know how to accompany voices, etc.

It is hardly by listening to masterpieces already known and consecrated, that an intelligent listener can discover who is to blame; but the number of these is so limited that their judgment is of little weight, and the bad conductor, before a public who would mercilessly hiss a fault on the part of a good singer, remains enthroned with all the

most position, and of whom both Wagner and Berlioz spoke with the warmest acknowledgment—that Habeneck of Paris, as Berlioz tells us, conducted not from the score but from a *violin part,* a custom to-day confined to beer-garden concerts with their waltzes and pot-pourris."— Ernest Newman's translation of Weingartner's " Ubas das Dirigieren " (Breitkopf and Härtel).

calmness possible, in all his dense ignorance and all his ineptitude.

Happily, I am here attacking an exception; the conductor, capable or otherwise, who is malevolent, is very rare.

On the contrary, the conductor of good-will, but who is incapable, is very common. Not to speak of innumerable mediocrities directing artists who are very often their superiors, an author, for example, could scarcely be accused of conspiring against his own work; yet there are those who, imagining they know how to conduct, innocently ruin their best scores.

Beethoven, it is said, more than once marred the execution of his symphonies, which he would conduct, even at the time when his deafness had become almost complete. The players, in order to keep together, agreed at last to follow the plain indications of movement given to them by the concert-meister (the principal first violin), and not to take any notice of Beethoven's baton. Yet it is well to know that the conducting of a symphony, an overture, or any other composition where the movements last for some time, varying little, and with no great difference of shading, is child's play in comparison with an opera or any other work containing recitatives, airs, and those numerous orchestral passages preceding untimed silences. The example of Beethoven just quoted leads me to say at once that if it seems to me difficult for a blind man to conduct an orchestra, it is beyond contradiction impossible for a deaf man, whatever may have been his technical ability before he lost his hearing.

The conductor should *see* and *understand*; he should be *agile* and *vigorous*; he should know the composition he conducts and the nature and extent of the instruments, he should know how to read a score, and should possess, in addition to the special talent and the constituent qualities we are about to explain, others* which are almost indefinable, and without which an impalpable barrier arises between him and those whom he directs, the faculty of transmitting to them his feelings is denied him, and therefore power and authority, the *directive* action, completely escapes him. He is no longer a chief, a director, but a mere wielder

---

* These "almost indefinable" qualities of a good conductor are well pointed out by Weingartner in the work above quoted. At page 11 he says: "The old flautist, Fürstenau of Dresden, told me that often, when Wagner conducted, the players had no sense of being led. Each believed himself to be following freely his own feeling, yet they all worked together wonderfully. It was Wagner's mighty will that powerfully but unperceived had overborne their single wills, so that each thought himself free, while in reality he only followed the leader, whose artistic force lived and worked in him."

2*

of the baton, a simple beater of time, even sup-
posing he knows how to beat and divide the time
properly.

It is essential that it should be felt that he feels,
that he understands, that he is, as it were, "pos-
sessed"; then his sentiment and his emotion com-
municate themselves to those whom he directs, the
internal fire escapes him, his electricity electrifies
them, the force of his impetus carries them away;
he projects all around him the burning rays of
the musical art. If, on the contrary, he is inert
and icy, he paralyses everybody before him, and
they become like masses of ice in a polar sea, the
approach of which is heralded by the chilliness of
the atmosphere.

The conductor's task is complex. He has not
only to direct, in the sense intended by the composer, a work of which a knowledge has already
been acquired by the executants, but also to con-
vey such knowledge to them in the case of a work
which is new to them. He has to criticise the
errors and faults of each of them during the rehearsals, and so to organise the resources at his
disposal as to get the best out of them as quickly
as possible; for in most of the cities of Europe
to-day, the musical art is so badly appreciated,
the executants are so badly paid, the need for
study is so little understood, that how to best em-

ploy time has to be reckoned amongst the most imperative demands of the conductor's art. We thus see in what consists the mechanical part of that art.

The capacity of the beater of time,* while it does not demand the highest musical abilities, is yet very difficult to acquire, and very few people really possess it. The signs which the conductor has to make, though generally simple, nevertheless become complicated in certain cases by the division and even the *subdivision* of the times of the movement.

The conductor, above all, is bound to possess a clear idea of the chief characteristics and points of the work which he has to direct at performance or at rehearsal, so that he may, without hesitation or mistake, determine from the outset what is wanted by the composer. If the conductor has not been able to receive instructions direct from the

---

* Wagner, in his book, "On Conducting," says: "The whole duty of a conductor is comprised in his ability always to indicate the right *tempo*," but this apparently arbitrary and somewhat deceptive dictum must not be too literally read, for he at once adds: "His choice of *tempi* will show whether he understands the piece or not." And this is the secret. The conductor's "ability always to understand the right *tempo*" involves a complete knowledge, understanding and appreciation of the music before him. And this, as Berlioz shows, makes of the real conductor a good deal more than a mere baton-waver (*see page 20 of the English translation by E. Dannreuther.* London: William Reeves).

composer, or if the right mode of performance has
not come down to him by tradition, he must have
recourse to the indications of the metronome, and
study well the numbers which most masters nowadays take care to write at the beginning and in
the course of their work.

I do not say that he should imitate the mathe-
matical regularity of the metronome; music executed in such fashion would be of arctic rigidity,
and I even doubt if it would be possible to maintain, during a certain number of bars, this dead
level of uniformity. But the metronome is none
the less excellent for giving the main time and the
principal changes.

In the absence of instructions from the composer, of tradition and of metronome marks, which
latter often happens with old works written at a
time when the metronome was not invented, there
are no other guides than the vague terms used to
indicate the pace of a work, and the feeling, more
or less fine and more or less correct, for the composer's style. We are bound to admit that these
guides are too often insufficient and deceptive.
One can convince oneself of this on seeing repre-
sented to-day the operas of the old repertoire in
places where the tradition of these works no longer
exists. Of any ten movements, at least four are
always taken in a contrary sense. I once heard

in a German theatre a chorus from "Iphigénie en Tauride," taken *allegro assai à deux temps* instead of *allegro non troppo à quatre temps*, which was exactly twice too fast. One might multiply indefinitely examples of similar disasters, brought about by the ignorance or carelessness of conductors, or else arising from the real difficulty experienced by the most gifted and careful men in finding out the exact meaning of the Italian words placed over movements.

Nobody, of course, will have any difficulty in distinguishing a *largo* from a *presto*. A conductor of small sagacity, if he examines the features and melodic designs of the piece, will soon arrive at the speed at which the composer meant a *presto* to go. But if a *largo* is of simple melodic construction, with only a small number of notes in each bar, what means has the unhappy conductor of discovering the true pace? And in how many ways may he not be mistaken! A great many degrees of slowness may be given to the execution of such a *largo*; the individual feeling of the conductor will thus be the only guide; and it is not his feeling, but that of the author, which matters. Composers ought therefore not to neglect to put metronome marks to their works, and conductors would then be bound to study them; to neglect such study would be dishonest.

I will now suppose the conductor to be perfectly instructed as to the pace of the work the performance or the rehearsal of which he is about to direct; he wishes to impart to the performers placed under his direction the rhythmical feeling which is in him, to fix the duration of each bar, and to make that duration uniformly observed by all the executants. Then that precision and that uniformity can only be secured from all the members of orchestra and choir by means of certain signs made by the conductor.

These signs will show the principal divisions, the *time* of the bar, and, in most cases, the subdivisions, the *half-time*. I need not explain here what is meant by the strong beat and the weak beat; I assume I am speaking to musicians.

The conductor generally uses a small light baton, of about half a metre in length,* and white rather than coloured because it can be better seen, which he holds in his right hand, so as to render easily appreciable his method of marking the beginning, the internal division, and the end of the bar. The bow used by some violinist conductors is not so suitable as the baton. It is somewhat flexible; its want of rigidity, and the resistance

---

* The French metre is equal to 39.36 inches; the length of baton mentioned by Berlioz would therefore be about nineteen and a half inches.—*Translator*.

which it offers to the air on account of the hair, cause its indications to be less precise.

The most simple of all times, the bar of two beats, is also very simply beaten.

The arm and the baton of the conductor being lifted so that his hand is on a level with his head, he marks the first beat by lowering the point of the baton perpendicularly (by the *bending of the wrist* as far as possible, and not by lowering the entire arm); and the second beat is marked by raising the baton perpendicularly by the contrary movement, thus:

Fig. 1.

The time of one beat in a bar being in reality, especially for the conductor, only a bar of two extremely rapid beats, should be done like the preceding. The necessity for the conductor to raise the point of his baton after lowering it, of course, divides that bar into two parts.

In time of four beats in a bar, the first move ment made from above to below (↓) is especiall adopted to strongly mark the first beat, the com mencement of the bar. The second movement made by the baton from right to left by raising it (↑), marks the second beat (first weak beat .

A third, transversely from left to right (⇒→) marks the third beat (second strong beat), and a fourth, obliquely from below upwards marks the fourth beat. The whole of these four movements may be thus illustrated :

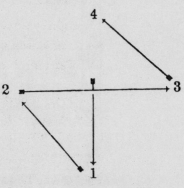

Fig. 2.

It is important that the conductor, in makin these movements in different directions, shoul move his arm but very little, and that the baton should therefore not go over a very large space, for each of these movements should be made almost instantaneously, or at any rate should take a moment so brief as to be inappreciable. If, on the contrary, that moment becomes appreciable, it ends, when multiplied by the number of times the movement has to be repeated, by putting the conductor behind the movement he wants to make, and by imparting to his work a most disagreeable sense of heaviness. This defect results moreover in uselessly tiring the conductor, and producing exaggerated and almost ridiculous evolutions which needlessly attract the attention of the audience and become painful to witness.

For three beats in a bar, the first movement, made from above to below, is also specially used to mark the first beat; but there are two ways of marking the second. Most conductors indicate it by a movement from left to right :

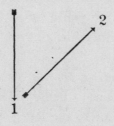

Fig. 3.

Some German conductors make the contrary
movement from right to left:

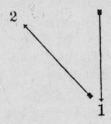

Fig. 4.

This latter movement has the disadvantage that,
when the chief turns his back to the orchestra, as
happens in the theatres, only a very small number
of the musicians are able to see this important
second beat, the body of the chief hiding the
movement of his arm. The other way is best, as
the chief moves his arm to the rear in taking it
away from his breast, and as his baton,
if he is careful to raise it a little above the
level of his shoulder, remains in full view of all
eyes.

When the chief faces his executants, it is a
matter of indifference whether he marks the second
beat to the right or to the left.

In any case, the third beat of three-in-a-bar

time is always marked like the last in four-in-
a-bar time, by an oblique upward movement,
thus :

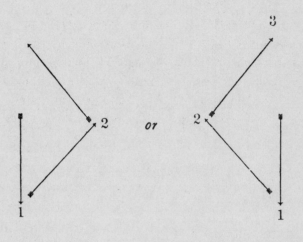

Fig. 5.   Fig. 6.

Five and seven beats in a bar will be better understood by the executants, if, instead of making a
series of special movements, they are treated, the
former as consisting of three beats and two, and
the latter of four and three.

The beats will therefore be thus marked :

Five beats :

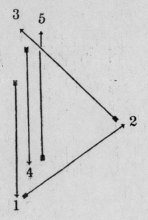

Fig. 7.

Seven beats :

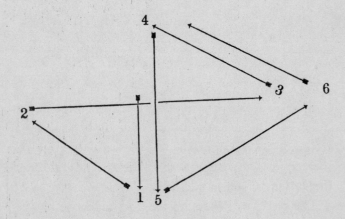

Fig. 8.

These different measures, divided in this way, are supposed to belong to modern movements. It is just the same whether the pace is very rapid or very slow.

Two in a bar, I have already explained, cannot be beaten otherwise than as we have seen in its place, however rapid it may be. But in case of its being too slow, the conductor should subdivide it.

A very quick four-in-a-bar time, on the contrary, should be beaten in two time; the four movements used in moderate time would then become so rapid that nothing precise would be presented to the eye, and the executants would be perplexed rather than helped. Moreover, and this is more serious, the chief, by uselessly making the four strokes in a rapid movement, makes it difficult to follow the rhythm, and loses the liberty of movement which the simple division of the time allows him.

Composers are generally wrong when in such cases they indicate four time. When the movement is very rapid this sign ₵ should always be written, and not this C, which will only lead the conductor astray.

The above remarks apply equally to very rapid three-time, $\frac{3}{4}$ or $\frac{3}{8}$. It is in these cases necessary

2

to suppress the movement for the second beat of
the bar, and remain a little longer on the stroke
of the first beat, lifting the baton only at the
third, thus :

Fig. 9.

It would be ridiculous to beat three strokes in
a bar in a Beethoven scherzo.

The opposite takes place for these two bars to
that for those of two beats. If the movement is
very slow, it is necessary to divide each time, and
therefore to make eight movements for the four-
beat bar, and six for the three-beat bar, repeating
and shortening each of the principal movements
which we have indicated above.

Example in very slow four time :

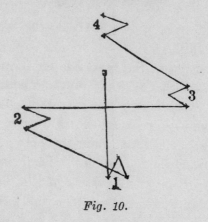

Fig. 10.

Example in very slow three time:

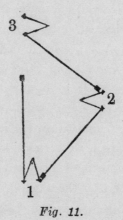

Fig. 11.

The arm should not at all partake in the little supplementary movement which we have indicated for the subdivision of the beat, the wrist only moving the baton.

This division of the beats has for its object the prevention of the different rhythms which might easily be set up among the executants during the interval which separates one beat from another. For as the conductor indicates nothing during that period, which becomes quite considerable owing to the extreme slowness of the movement, the executants are then left entirely to themselves, *without a leader*, and as the rhythmical feeling is not the same with all, it follows that some would press forward while others held back, and the *ensemble* would soon be destroyed. An exception to this rule can only be made in conducting an orchestra of the very first order, composed of virtuosos who know each other well, are in the habit of always playing together, and who know almost by heart the music which they play. And even under these conditions, the inattention of one single player may lead to an accident. Why run the risk? I know that the vanity of some artists is easily wounded by their being " kept in leading strings like children," as they call it; but this consideration has no weight with a chief who keeps in view nothing but the excellence of the final result. Even in a quartet it is very rare to find the individual feeling of the executants free from a desire to " let itself go "; in a symphony it is the feeling of the conductor which matters; the perfection of execution consists in understanding and reproducing the *ensemble*; individual desires, which moreover do not agree amongst themselves, cannot be allowed to be manifested.

This being admitted, it will easily be understood that subdivision is still more essential in very slow movements, such as $\frac{6}{4}$, $\frac{6}{8}$, $\frac{9}{8}$, $\frac{12}{8}$, etc.

But these times, where the ternary rhythm plays so important a rôle, may be divided up in several ways.

If the movement is quick or moderate, it is hardly necessary to do more than indicate the simple beats of these bars according to the method adopted for analogous simple measures.

Allegretto $\frac{6}{8}$ and *allegro* $\frac{6}{4}$ will thus be beaten as if in two time : ¢, 2, or $\frac{2}{4}$; $\frac{9}{8}$ will be marked like $\frac{3}{4}$ *moderato*, or $\frac{3}{8}$ *andantino*; $\frac{12}{8}$ *moderato* or *allegro*, like simple four-time. But if the movement is *adagio, largo assai* or *andante maestoso*, it should be marked, according to the form of the melody and the predominant design, either on all the quavers, or by one crotchet followed by a quaver for each beat.

Fig. 12.

It is not necessary at each beat in three-time, to mark all the quavers; the rhythm of a crotchet followed by a quaver at each beat is enough.

The little movement indicater should always be used for subdivision in simple measures; but this subdivision will at each beat be divided into two unequal parts, as it will indicate to the eye the value of the crotchet and of the quaver.

If the movement is still slower, there must be no hesitation, and it is only possible to secure the *ensemble* in execution by marking every quaver, no matter what is the nature of the composition.

Fig. 13.

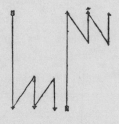

In these three times, at the pace indicated, the conductor will mark three quavers per beat, three down and three up for $\frac{6}{8}$:

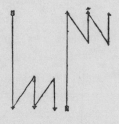

Fig. 14.

three down, and three to the right and three up, for $\frac{9}{8}$:

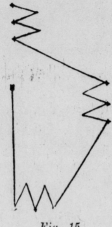

Fig. 15.

and three down, three to the left, three to the right and three above, for $\frac{12}{8}$:

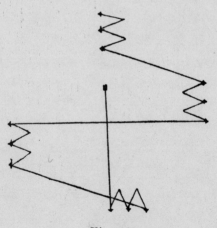

Fig. 16.

A difficult problem sometimes presents itself, viz., when in a score certain parts, for the purpose of contrast are written in three rhythm while the other parts preserve the two rhythm :

Fig. 17.

No doubt if the part for the wind instruments in this example is confided to musicians who are *real* musicians, there will be no need to change the method of beating the time, and the conductor may continue to subdivide into six or simply to divide into two; but as most executants seem to hesitate at the moment when, by the use of the syncopated form, the ternary rhythm intervenes with the binary rhythm and they become mixed, here are the means of giving them confidence. The inquietude caused to them by the sudden appearance of this unexpected rhythm, which is opposed to the rest of the orchestra, instinctively leads the players to cast an eye on the chief, as though to ask for his help. He ought then to look at them, turn a little towards them, and mark the ternary rhythm by very small movements, as if the measure was really in three time, so that the violins and the other instruments playing in binary rhythm may not notice the change, which would put them out entirely. The result of this compromise is that the new ternary rhythm, being marked secretly by the chief, will be executed with assurance, while the binary rhythm, already firmly established, will continue without trouble, although the chief does not mark it.

On the other hand nothing, in my opinion, is more blameable, and more contrary to good musical sense, than the application of this method to passages where there is no superposition of two rhythms of opposed kinds, and where there is only the use of syncopation. The chief, dividing the bar by *the number of accents which it is found to contain*, destroys the effect of the syncopated form for all who see him, and substitutes a rapid change of measure for a rhythmic play of the most piquant interest. That is what happens if the accents instead of the time are marked in the following passage from Beethoven's " Pastoral " Symphony :

Fig. 18.

and if the six movements indicated are made instead of the four previously established, which
allow the syncopation to be seen and better felt :

Fig. 19.

This voluntary offering of a rhythmical form
which the author intended to be different is one
of the worst faults of style of which a beater of
time can be guilty.

Another sort of difficulty which presents itself
to the conductor, and for which he needs all his
presence of mind, is the superposition of different
times. It is easy to conduct a passage of two beats
binary time placed over or under another passage
of two time ternary, if both are in the same movement; they are then equal in duration, and it is
only a question of dividing them in the middle by
marking the two principal times.

Fig. 20.

But if in the middle of a piece of slow movement, a new form of quick movement is introduced, and if the composer, either to render the execution of the quick movement easier, or because it was impossible to write otherwise, adopts for the new movement the short time which corresponds to it, there may be two or even three quick times superimposed upon a slow one, thus:

Fig. 21.

No. 1.

No. 2.
(Three beats against one).

No. 3

The task of the conductor is to make to go together and to maintain the *ensemble* of various times in unequal numbers, and in dissimilar movements. In the preceding example he will begin to divide the beat of the measure *andante* No. 1 which precedes the entry of the allegro in $\frac{6}{8}$, and continue to divide them, but taking care, however, to mark this division. The executants of the *allegro* in $\frac{6}{8}$ will then understand that the two movements of the chief represent the two beats of their small measure, and the executants of the *andante* that the same two movements represent for them only a part divided from their larger passage.

Measure No. 1 :

Fig. 22.

Measures No. 2, 3, etc. :

Fig. 23.

It will be seen that this is really very simple,
because the division of the small measure and the
subdivisions of the large measure coincide with
each other. The following example, where a slow
measure is superposed on two short measures,
without that coincidence existing, is more
perilous :

Fig. 24.

Allegretto.

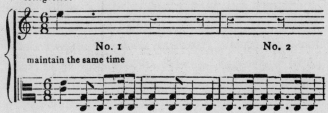

No. 1   No. 2

maintain the same time

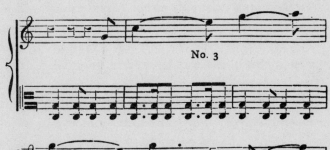

No. 3

Here the three bars *allegro assai* which precede the *allegretto*, will each have two simple beats as usual. At the moment when the *allegro* begins, the bar of which is double that of the preceding and of that taken by the violas, the chief marks two time divided, for the large bar, by two unequal motions below and two above:

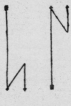

Fig. 25.

The two large motions divide the large bar in the middle, and make their value understood by the oboes, without disturbing the violas who take the quick movement, on account of the small motion

which also divides their small bar in the middle.
From bar No. 3 he will thus cease to divide the
large bar by four, on account of the ternary
rhythm of the melody in $\frac{6}{8}$ which that division
opposes. He then begins to mark the two time of
the large bar, and the violas, already started on
their rapid rhythm, continue it without trouble,
understanding quite well that each movement of
the conductor's baton marks only the commence-
ment of their small bar.

And this last remark makes it clear with what
care it is necessary to be exact to divide the beats
of a bar when one part of the orchestra or the
voices, come to execute triplets on those beats.
This division thus cutting in half the second note
of the triplet might make the execution unsteady,
and might damage it altogether. It is even necessary to abstain from this division of the beats of
the bar by two, a little before the moment when
the rhythmic or melodic design comes to divide
them by three, in order not to give to the executants in advance the feeling of a rhythm contrary
to that which they want to be heard.

4

Fig. 26.

In this example the subdivision of the bar by
six, or the division of the beat by two, is useful,
and causes no inconvenience during bar one; the
following motions are then made :

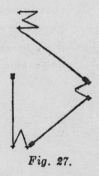

Fig. 27.

but it is necessary to abstain from the opening of
bar two, and return to the simple movement

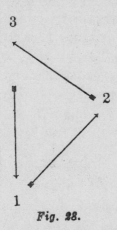

Fig. 28.

because of the triplet coming on the third beat,
and because of the following, which the double
motion would greatly disturb.

In the famous ball scene from Mozart's "Don
Giovanni," the difficulty of making the three orchestras written in three different measures is less
than might be believed. It is enough to always
mark each beat of the *tempo di minuetto* with a
downward motion.

Fig. 29.

Once entered on the ensemble, the little allegretto in ⅜ and the other allegro in ¾, agree perfectly with the chief theme, and go without the least embarrassment.

A great fault which I have seen committed consists in spreading out the bar of a piece in two time when the author has introduced a triplet of minims:

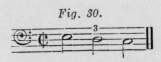

Fig. 30.

In such a case the third minim adds nothing to the duration of the bar, as some conductors seem to think. One may, if one chooses, and if the movement is slow or moderate, mark these passages by beating three time, but the duration of the whole bar remains exactly the same. In the case where these triplets encounter a bar in two time *(allegro assai)* the three motions make confusion, and it is absolutely necessary to make only two, one on the first minim and up again on the third. These motions, on account of the quickness of the movement, differ little to the eye from those of the bar of two equal beats, and do not interfere with the progress of those parts of the orchestra which have no triplets.

Fig. 31.

We spoke above of the action of the conductor in recitatives. Here the reciting singer or instrumentalist, being more submissive to the regular division of the bar, it is a question, by following him attentively, of making the orchestra attack with precision and unity the chords or instrumental passages with which the recitative is intermingled, and of making the suitable changes in the harmony when the recitative is accompanied, either by holding notes, or by a tremolo in several parts of which the most obscure is that to which the conductor ought to pay great attention, seeing that it is from the movement of these that changes of chord result.

Fig. 32.

In this example the conductor, in following the unmeasured recitative, has to concern himself particularly with the viola part, and to cause it to move suitably from the first beat to the second, from the F to the E at the beginning of the second bar; without this, as this part is played by several instruments in unison, some will hold on the F longer than others, and result in discord.

Some conductors, when conducting an orchestra with recitatives, are in the habit of taking no account of the written division of the bar, and of marking an up beat before that on which occurs the brief chord struck by the orchestra, even when that chord is placed on a weak beat.

Fig. 33.

In such a passage they lift the arm on the crotchet beat which begins the bar, and lower it on the chord beat. I cannot approve of such a usage, which nothing can justify, and which may often lead to accidents in performance.

I do not, moreover, know why, in recitatives,

they should cease to divide the bar regularly, and to mark the real beats in their places, just as in measured music. I therefore advise, in the preceding example, that the first beat be made downwards as usual, and to take the baton to the left to attack the chord on the second beat; and to follow this plan in all analogous cases, and divide the bar regularly. It is, further, very important to divide according to the preceding pace indicated by the author, and not to forget, if the movement is allegro or maestoso, and if the reciting part has gone on some time without accompaniment, to give to the time, when the orchestra re-enters, the value of an allegro or maestoso. For when the orchestra plays alone it is in general time; it does not play without time when it accompanies the reciting voice or instrument. In the exceptional case where the recitative is written for the orchestra itself, or for the chorus, or even for a part of the orchestra or chorus, it is a question of making a certain number of executants go together, whether in unison or in harmony, but in exact time, *it is then the conductor who is the real reciter*, and who gives to each beat of the bar the duration which he judges suitable. Following the form of the phrase, he will now divide and subdivide the time, now he will mark the accents, now the double quavers, and finally he will show

with his baton the melodic form of the recitative.
It is well understood that the executants, knowing
their notes nearly by heart, will keep their eyes
constantly fixed on him, for without this neither
certainty nor ensemble will be possible.

In general, even for measured music, the conductor should demand that the executants look at
him as often as possible. *For an orchestra which
does not look at the conductor's baton has no
leader.* Frequently, after a pause, for example, the
conductor is obliged to abstain from making the
decisive movement which fixes the attack of the
orchestra, until he sees the eyes of all the musicians fixed upon himself. It is for the chief to
accustom them, during rehearsals, to look at him
at the important moment.

Fig. 34.

If in the above passage where there is a pause,
perhaps indefinitely prolonged on the first beat,
the rule I have just pointed out is not observed,
the passage:

Fig. 35.

cannot be thrown out with promptitude, the players who do not look at the conductor's baton cannot know when he takes up the second beat and resumes the movement suspended by the pause.

This obligation for the executants to look at their conductor necessarily implies the obligation on him to allow himself to be seen by all of them. Whatever the disposition of the orchestra, whether on the slope or on a level, he should arrange so as to be himself the centre of all the visual rays.

In order to raise himself, and keep himself in view, the conductor should stand on an elevated platform, which should be higher in proportion to the number of the executants and the space they occupy. His desk should not be high enough for the board on which the score is laid to hide his figure, for the expression of his face stands for much in the influence which he exercises.

The making of any noise whatever, either by the conductor's baton on the desk or by the foot on the platform, is to be unreservedly condemned. It is worse than a bad habit—it is a barbarism.

But if, in a theatre, the evolutions on the stage

prevent the chorus from seeing the conductor's baton, the conductor must, to ensure the attack of the chorus after a silence, give a light tap on the desk with his baton. This exceptional case is the only one which justifies the employment of any indicating noise, and it is to be regretted that even this expedient has to be resorted to.

On this question of the chorus and their action in theatres, it is as well to say here that the directors of the singing often have to mark the beat behind the scenes, and sometimes without even hearing the orchestra. From this it results that this arbitrary beat, done more or less badly, cannot agree with that of the chief, and inevitably sets up a rhythmical discord between the chorus and the instrumental group, and instead of helping to establish the ensemble, tends to upset it.

There is another traditional barbarism which it is the business of the intelligent and energetic conductor to destroy. If a chorus or an instrumental piece has to be executed behind the scenes without the participation of the principal orchestra, another conductor is absolutely necessary to conduct it. If the orchestra accompanies this group, the first conductor, who hears the music from afar, is bound to *leave it to be conducted by the second*, and to follow the movements *by ear*. But if, as is often the case in modern music, the sonority of the chief orchestra prevents the chief conductor from hearing what is going on at a distance, the introduction of a special mechanical conductor of the rhythm becomes indispensable, in order to establish an instantaneous communication between him and the distant performers. Several more or less ingenious attempts have been made in this direction, of which the result has not always been what was expected. That in the Covent Garden Theatre, London, which was moved by the foot of the conductor, worked very well. But the *electric metronome*, installed by Mr. Verbrugghe in the Brussels Theatre, leaves nothing to be desired.* It consists of an apparatus made of copper wire, starting from a Volta pile placed below, connected with the chief's desk, and ending at a movable baton, one end of which works on a pivot, in front of a board placed *at any distance from the chief conductor*. A brass key, something like a pianoforte key, is fitted to the chief conductor's desk, with a short projection fitted on its lower surface. Directly below this projection is a cup, also of brass, and filled with mercury. At the moment when the conductor, wishing to mark any beat in

---

* The reader will remember here and throughout this little work that Berlioz wrote in 1856.—*Translator*.

the bar, presses down this key with the index finger
of his left hand (the right being, as usual, employed by holding the baton), the lowering of the
key sends the projection into the cup of mercury,
a feeble spark is emitted, and the baton placed at
the other end of the copper wire makes a motion
in front of the board. This communication of
fluid and the movement are absolutely instantaneous, whatever be the distance traversed.   The executants grouped behind the scenes, with their eyes
fixed on the electric metronome, are directly under
the control of the chief, who can, if necessary,
direct from the middle of the orchestra of the Paris
Opéra a piece of music performed at Versailles.*
It is only important to note that it must be arranged with the choir or with their conductor (if
from excess of caution one is employed) how the
chief conductor marks the movement—whether he
marks all the principal beats or only the first beat,
seeing that the oscillations of the baton moved by
electricity are simply down and up, and indicate
nothing precise in this respect.

When I used for the first time at Brussels the
valuable instrument which I have attempted to
describe, its use had one inconvenience.   Every

---

* Berlioz might have added, " or in London or Lyons."—
Translator.

time the brass key on my desk was pressed down
by the index finger of my left hand, it struck
against another piece of brass below; and in spite
of the delicacy of this contact, a small noise re-
sulted, which during the silence of the orchestra
attracted the attention of the audience to the detri-
ment of the musical effect. I pointed out this defect to Mr. Verbrugghe, who replaced the lower
piece of brass by the cup filled with mercury of
which I spoke above, in which the upper projection
introduced itself to set up the electric current
without making the least noise.

In connection with this mechanism it now only
remains to do away with the crackling of the spark
at the moment of breaking the current—a crackling too weak to be heard by the public.

This metronome is not expensive to set up; it
costs about four hundred francs (£16). The large
theatres, concert halls and churches have long been
provided with it. The usefulness of Mr. Verbrugghe's invention became evident at the large
concerts which I directed last year (1855) at the
Palace of the Universal Industrial Exhibition—
concerts at which there were more than a thousand
performers, who executed pieces in very rapid time
with such astonishing precision and irreproachable
ensemble that three of the lyric theatres of Paris
(the Théâtre Italien, the Opéra Comique and the

Théâtre Lyrique) each installed an electric metronome without delay.

I have not yet spoken of those dangerous auxiliaries who are called directors of choirs. Few of them are really sufficiently able to conduct a musical performance so that the conductor can depend upon them. The most dangerous of them are those whose age has destroyed their agility and energy. The keeping up of any quick movement is impossible to them. Whatever be the rapidity with which a movement confided to them may begin, little by little they slacken off, until the rhythm is reduced to a slow pace in harmony with the movement of their blood and the enfeeblement of their organism. It is only fair to say that these old men are not the only ones who induce this danger to composers. There are men, at the flower of their age, who are of a lymphatic temperament, and whose blood seems to circulate moderato. If they have to direct an allegro assai, they gradually slow it down to a moderato; if, on the other hand, it is a largo or an andante sostenuto, it is slowly hurried up until it becomes a moderato long before the close. The moderato is their natural movement; and they come back to it as infallibly as a hastened or retarded pendulum as soon as it is released. Such people are the born enemies of all musical character, and the levellers down of style.

May all conductors be protected from their help at any cost!

One day, in a large city which I will not mention, it was necessary to perform behind the scenes a very simple chorus in $\frac{6}{8}$ time, allegretto. The help of the chorus conductor became essential; he was an old man. The movement of the chorus being at first fixed by the orchestra, our Nestor followed all right for the first few bars; but shortly afterwards the slowing down became so marked that it was not possible to keep on without rendering the piece completely ridiculous. It was begun again the second time, the third time, the fourth time; half-an-hour was wasted in more and more irritating attempts, and always with the same result. The keeping up of the movement to allegretto was absolutely impossible to this good soul. At last the impatient chief conductor begged him not to conduct at all; he had found a way out of the difficulty; he made the choristers imitate a march movement, lifting each foot in turn without changing position. This movement being in exact relation with the binary rhythm of the $\frac{6}{8}$ time in allegretto, the choristers, no longer hampered by their conductor, at once performed the piece by singing in march time with ensemble and regularity, and without slowing down.

I admit, however, that many chorus masters or

sub-conductors are sometimes of real use, and even indispensable in maintaining the ensemble of large masses of performers. When these masses are of necessity so placed that part of them have their backs turned towards the chief conductor, the latter will then need a number of under beaters of time placed in front of those performers who cannot see the chief conductor, and who will reproduce all his movements. In order that this reproduction of beats may be precise, the subordinate time-beaters must never for a single moment take their eyes off the chief conductor. If, in order to look at their books, they fail to see him for even three beats only, a discord will occur between their beats and his, and all is lost.

At a festival where twelve hundred performers were united under my direction, in Paris, in 1844, I had to employ five choir directors placed amongst the vocal body, and two under-conductors for the orchestra, one of whom directed the wind instruments and the other the instruments of percussion. I bade them look at me without ceasing, and not to forget to do so; and our eight batons raised and lowered without the slightest difference of rhythm, established among our twelve hundred performers the most perfect ensemble, such as had never before been known. But now, with one or several electric metronomes, it does not seem necessary to resort to such means. As a matter of fact, one can, without trouble, direct choristers whose backs are turned towards the conductor. Yet in some cases attentive and intelligent sub-conductors will always be preferable to a machine.

They have not only to beat the time, like a metronomic baton, but they have also to speak to the groups under their control, to call their attention to light and shade, and, after silences, to point out the moment of re-entry.

In a building arranged as a semi-amphitheatre, the conductor can alone conduct a considerable number of performers, being able, without trouble, to always keep their eyes fixed on him. Nevertheless, the use of a number of sub-conductors seems to me to be preferable to one single individual director, because of the great distance of the extremes of the vocal and instrumental masses from himself. The greater the distance which separates the conductor from those whom he directs, the more is his action enfeebled. The best plan seems to be to have several sub-conductors, with several electric metronomes beating before their eyes the main beats of the bar. It was in this way that I directed, in 1855, the concerts at the Exhibition.

Now, ought the conductor to conduct standing or sitting? If, in a theatre, where scores of enormous length have to be played, it is very difficult

to resist fatigue when standing the whole evening,
it is none the less true that the conductor, when
seated, loses part of his power, and cannot give
free play to his energy, if he has any. Should
he conduct from a large score or by playing the
first violin, as is the custom in some theatres? It
is evident that he should have a full score before
him to conduct from. To lead from a part containing only the principal instrumental entries, the
bass and the melody, imposes on the conductor's
memory a useless task, and exposes him, moreover, in case he should have to speak to one of the
players whose part is not before him, to the reply,
"What do you know about it?"

The disposal and the grouping of players and
singers is the business of the conductor, especially
at concerts. It is impossible to state in one sen-
tence the best grouping of the performers in a
theatre and in a concert hall, as the form and arrangement of the interior necessarily influence the
arrangements to be made in such cases. We may
further add that these arrangements depend on
the number of performers to be grouped, and, on
some occasions, on the kind of composition
adopted by the author. Speaking generally as to
concerts, an amphitheatre of eight, or at least five,
stages is indispensable.

For this amphitheatre the semicircular form is

best. If it is large enough to hold the entire orchestra, the first violins should be in front on the
right, the second violins in front on the left; the
violas in the middle between the two violin groups;
the flutes, oboes, clarinets, horns and bassoons
behind the first violins; a double rank of violoncellos and double basses behind the second violins;
the trumpets, trombones and tubas behind the
violas; the rest of the violoncellos and double
basses behind the wood-wind; the harps in front of
all, close to the conductor; the drums and other
instruments of percussion behind the brass; the
conductor's back should be towards the public, at
the bottom of the amphitheatre and close to the
desks of the first and second violins.

There should be a horizontal platform, of greater
or lesser size, extending in front of the first stage
of the amphitheatre: on this platform the choristers will be placed in fan-like form, three parts
turned towards the public, and all able to easily
see the conductor. The grouping of the singers
according to class of voice will vary as the author
has written for three, four, or six parts. In all
cases the ladies, sopranos and contraltos, will be
in front, seated; the tenors behind the contraltos,
and the basses behind the sopranos.

The solo singers and players will occupy the
centre in front of all, and will always be placed

so as to be able, by a slight turn of the head, to see the baton of the conductor.

These indications are only approximate, and they may, for many reasons, be modified in various ways.

At the Paris Coservatoire, where the amphi-theatre consists of only four or five stages, not cir-cular, and which therefore cannot hold all the orchestra, the violins and violas are in front, the basses and wind instruments alone occupy the stages; the chorus is seated in front facing the public, and the entire group of lady sopranos and contraltos have their backs to the conductor, and can never see his movements. This arrangement is very inconvenient for that part of the chorus.

It is of the highest importance that the choristers placed in front should be on a lower plane than the violins, as without this the latter would be enormously reduced in sonority. For the same reason, if there are no other stages in front for the chorus, it is absolutely necessary that the ladies should be seated and the men remain standing, so that the tenor and bass voices, starting from a higher point than that of the sopranos and con-traltos, may be emitted freely and not muffled or intercepted.

When the presence of the choristers in front of the orchestra is no longer required the conductor should make them retire, as such a crowd of human bodies would damage the sonority of the instruments. A symphony performed by a more or less muffled orchestra would suffer much.

There are still some precautions in regard to the orchestra itself which the chief can take so as to avoid certain defects in execution.

The instruments of percussion, placed, as I have said, on one of the rear stages of the amphitheatre, are apt to retard the rhythm and to get behind. A series of blows on the big drum struck at regular intervals in a quick movement, thus:

Fig. 36.

Allegro.

sometimes lead to the complete destruction of a beautiful rhythmical progression by breaking the "go" of the rest of the orchestra and destroying the ensemble. Nearly always the player of the big drum, failing to regard the first beat marked by the conductor, gets a little behind in making the first stroke. This delay, multiplied by the number of strokes which follow the first, very quickly leads to a disagreement of the most damaging kind.

The conductor, whose efforts are to re-establish the ensemble in such a case, has only one thing left to do, viz., to demand that the player of the big drum should count in advance the number of strokes he has to make in the passage in question, and, knowing this, should no longer look at his book, but keep his eyes fixed on the conductor's baton; he will then soon be able to follow the movement without the least lack of precision. Another delay, arising from a different cause, is often noticed in the trumpet parts, when they contain in a rapid movement passages such as this:

Fig. 37.

Allegro

The trumpet player, instead of breathing *before* the first of these three bars, breathes at the beginning, on the quaver rest A, and, not taking into account the small time he has for breathing, nevertheless gives all that time to the quaver which is thus superadded to the first bar, which results in the following effect:

Fig. 38.

Allegro.

a result which is so much the worse on account of the final accent, struck at the beginning of the third bar by the rest of the orchestra, comes a third of the time too late with the trumpets, and destroys the ensemble of the attack on the last chord.

To obviate this, the conductor should, first of all, in advance, call the attention of the performers to this mistake into which they are all likely to fall, and then, when conducting the passage, turn his eye upon them at the decisive moment, and *anticipate a little* in striking the first beat of the bar in which they enter. One would hardly believe how difficult it is to prevent the trumpet players from doubling the value of a quaver thus placed.

When a long *accellerando a poco a poco* is indicated by the composer to reach a *presto* from an allegro moderato, most conductors press on the movement *by jerks*, instead of always insensibly getting faster. This is to be carefully avoided. The same remark applies to the inverse proceeding. It is even more difficult to bring down steadily a rapid movement without any jerkiness, so as to transform it little by little into a slow movement.

A conductor, to show his zeal, or from a lack of delicacy in his musical feeling, will often demand from his performers *exaggerated shading*.

He understands neither the character nor the style of the piece. The shades then become spots, and the accents screeches; the intentions of the poor composer are utterly disfigured and perverted, and those of the conductor are no less unfortunate, like the ass in the fable, whose master beat him to death while caressing him.

We will now point out several deplorable abuses common in nearly all the orchestras in Europe— abuses which drive composers to despair, and which it is the duty of conductors to abolish as soon as possible.

Artists who play bowed instruments will rarely give themselves the trouble to play a tremolo; they substitute for that characteristic effect a dull repetition of the note, half, and often three-fourths slower than that resulting from the tremolo; instead of four quavers they will play triplets, or even crotchets; instead of producing sixty-four notes in a bar of four time (adagio) they only produce thirty-two, or even sixteen. The quivering of the arm required to produce a true tremolo is no doubt very fatiguing! But this laziness is intolerable. A large number of double bass players, from sheer idleness, or through fear of not being able to conquer certain difficulties, simplify their parts. This school of simplifiers, which has been in honour for forty years, should no longer be

allowed to exist. In the old works the double
bass parts are very simple; there is no reason to
impoverish them any further; those of modern
scores are, it is true, a little more difficult, but,
with very rare exceptions, they are not unplayable;
the composers, masters of their business, write them
with care, and so that they can be played. If it
is from idleness that the simplifiers denaturalise
these parts, the energetic conductor is armed with
authority to make them do their duty. If it is
from incapacity, he can dismiss them. He has
every interest in getting rid of players who cannot
play their instruments.

Flute players, accustomed to dominate the other
wind instruments, and not admitting that their part
may be written below those of the oboes and clarinets, frequently transpose entire passages a whole
octave upwards. The chief, if he does not read his
score, if he does not thoroughly know the work
which he is directing, or if his ear is lacking in
delicacy, does not perceive this strange liberty
taken by the flautists. These things ought to be
altogether abolished.

It happens everywhere (I do not say in some
orchestras only), it happens everywhere, I repeat,
that ten, fifteen, or twenty violinists, having to
execute the same part in unison, do not count their
rests, but depend upon each other, through idle-

ness. Hence it happens that scarcely half of them come in at the right moment, while the other half hold their instruments under their left arms and look at the ceiling; the entry is thus enfeebled, if not totally ruined. I call down upon this insufferable habit the attention and the severest censure of conductors. It is nevertheless so deep-rooted that it can only be got rid of by fining a large number of players for the fault of one; for instance, the whole of one row if one of their number has failed to enter at the right moment. When this fine is only three francs, and it may be inflicted on the same player five or six times at one sitting, I reply that each player will count his rests, and not rely upon his neighbour.

An orchestra in which the instruments are not in tune with each other, and each one singly, is a monstrosity; the chief will therefore take the greatest care that the performers are all in tune. But that process should not be carried out before the public. Moreover, all instrumental noise, and all preluding between the entr'actes constitutes a real offence to a civilised audience. The bad education and the musical mediocrity of a orchestra are recognised by noises heard during the moments of silence in an opera or a concert.

It is incumbent upon a conductor to see that the

clarinettists do not always use the same instrument (say the B flat clarinet) without regard to
the indications of the author. Different clarinets
have a special character the value of which is well
known to the composer; the clarinet in A is also
half a tone lower than that in B flat, and the
C sharp has an excellent effect:

Fig. 39.

produced by this note:

Fig. 40.

which E only gives D:

Fig. 41.

on the clarinet in B flat.

A habit as vicious, and still more pernicious, is

the introduction in many orchestras of horns with cylinders and pistons, and to play on these, *in open notes*, by means of the new mechanism fitted to the instrument, notes intended by the composer to be produced as *closed notes* by inserting the right hand in the bell. Many horn players nowadays, because of the facility afforded by the pistons or cylinders to put their instruments into various keys, only use the horn in F, whatever may be the key indicated by the composer. This habit leads to all sorts of inconveniences, from which the conductor should use all his efforts to guard the works of composers who know how to write; with regard to the rest it may be admitted that the evil is not so great.

He ought also to resist the economical practice adopted in some so-called lyric theatres, of letting the same man play the cymbals and the big drum. The tone of the cymbals when attached to the big drum, to make them as economical as possible, is an ignoble one, worthy only of second-rate dances. This custom, moreover, induces mediocre composers never to use alone one of these two instruments and not to use them as uniquely proper for the energetic accentuation of the strong beats of a bar.

In conclusion, I will express my regret to see everywhere the studies of the chorus and orchestra so badly organised. Everywhere, for grand compositions for chorus and orchestra, the plan of rehearing together is adhered to. Each should be rehearsed separately, the chorus at one time and the orchestra at another.

Deplorable errors, innumerable blunders, are thus committed, errors which the chorus master and the conductor do not see. Once these errors are established they become habits, which persistently introduce themselves at the performances. Moreover, the unhappy choristers are most badly treated. Instead of giving them *a good conductor* knowing the work, instructed in the art of singing, to beat the time and make critical observations; *a good pianist* playing a *well made pianoforte score on a good piano*; and a violinist to play in unison or in octaves each part when studied separately— instead of these three indispensable artists, they are entrusted, in three-fourths of the lyric theatres of Europe, to a man who has no more idea of conducting than he has of singing, generally a poor musician, selected from the poorest possible pianists, or rather who does not play the piano at all, seated before a shattered piano, taxed to decipher a dislocated score which he does not know, striking wrong chords, majors instead of minors, and vice versa, and, under the pretext of accompanying and conducting all by himself, and waving his right hand so as to lead the choristers to fail in the rhythm, and his left hand so as to ruin the intonation.

One might fancy one's self in the middle ages when he sees this economic barbarism.

A faithful, coloured and inspired interpretation of a modern work, confided to artists of a high order, can, I firmly believe, only be secured by separate rehearsals. It is necessary to study each part of a chorus by itself, until that part is well known, before admitting it to the collective body. The same rule is to be followed with the orchestra even for a tolerably easy symphony. The violins should first be rehearsed alone, then the violas and basses, then the wood-wind, with a small group of stringed instruments to fill up the rests and accustom the wood-wind to the re-entries, the like for the brass instruments; it is very often necessary to exercise the percussion instruments alone, and lastly the harps if there is a body of them. The work done in a body is thus rendered more fruitful and more rapid, and one may flatter one's self at arriving at a result which, alas! is proved to be but too rare.

The performances obtained under the old method are only of the "almost" sort, under which so many conductors succumb.*   The conductor-organiser, after the slaughter of a master, does not lay down his baton with a sigh of satisfaction; and if doubts lurk in his mind as to the way in which he has fulfilled his task, as, in the last analysis, nobody gave him any advice as to how to control its accomplishment, he murmurs to himself: "Bah! Woe to the vanquished!"

H. BERLIOZ.

* Weingartner's last paragraph comes in aptly here : "More and more I have come to think that what decides the worth of conducting is the degree of suggestive power that the conductor can exercise over the performers. . . . . It is not the transference of his personal will, but the mysterious act of creation that called the work into being takes place again in him, and transcending the narrow limits of reproduction, he becomes a new creator, a self-creator. *O si sic omnes!*